MAR   2021

SESAME STREET®

All about DOCTORS

Jennifer Boothroyd

Lerner Publications ◆ Minneapolis

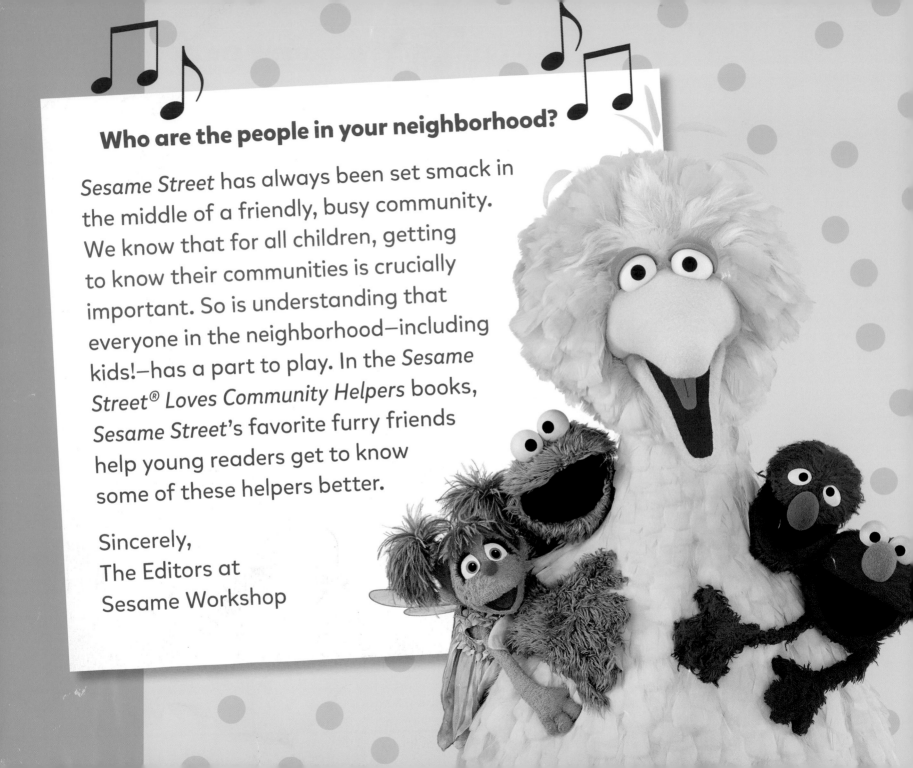

Who are the people in your neighborhood?

Sesame Street has always been set smack in the middle of a friendly, busy community. We know that for all children, getting to know their communities is crucially important. So is understanding that everyone in the neighborhood—including kids!—has a part to play. In the *Sesame Street® Loves Community Helpers* books, *Sesame Street*'s favorite furry friends help young readers get to know some of these helpers better.

Sincerely,
The Editors at
Sesame Workshop

Table of Contents

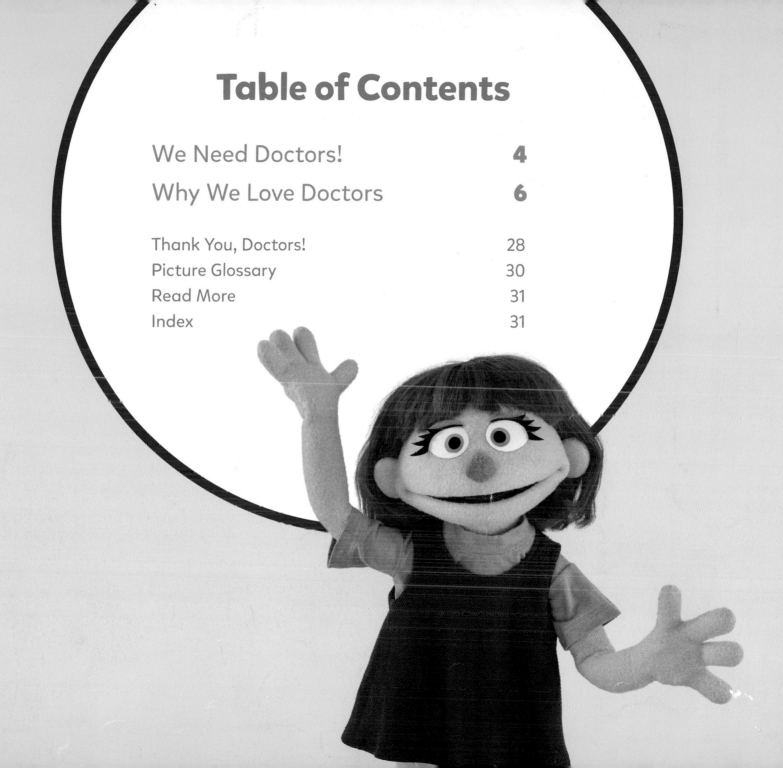

We Need Doctors!

I like to visit my doctor. Doctors make us healthy.

Why We Love Doctors

Doctors are community helpers. They work at clinics and hospitals.

A patient is the person seeing a doctor.

Patients wait for their turn.

Playing with toys makes waiting fun!

9

Sometimes patients are sick. Sometimes patients just need a checkup.

Doctors work with nurses. Nurses check how tall you are. They weigh you.

The nurse needs a step stool to see how tall I am.

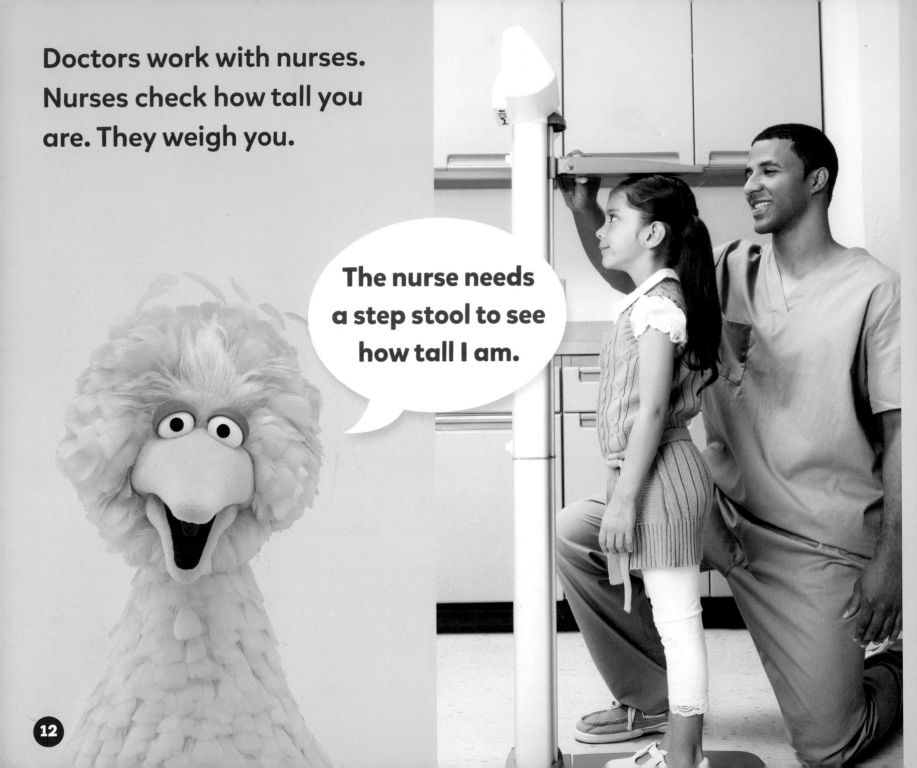

Special clothes keep doctors and patients safe.

Many doctors wear a white coat.

Sometimes doctors wear gloves.

A patient sits on a table in the room.

Doctors listen to your heart. They listen to your breathing.

Doctors look inside your ears. They look inside your mouth.

Saying *BLAAAH* is the best part of visiting the doctor.

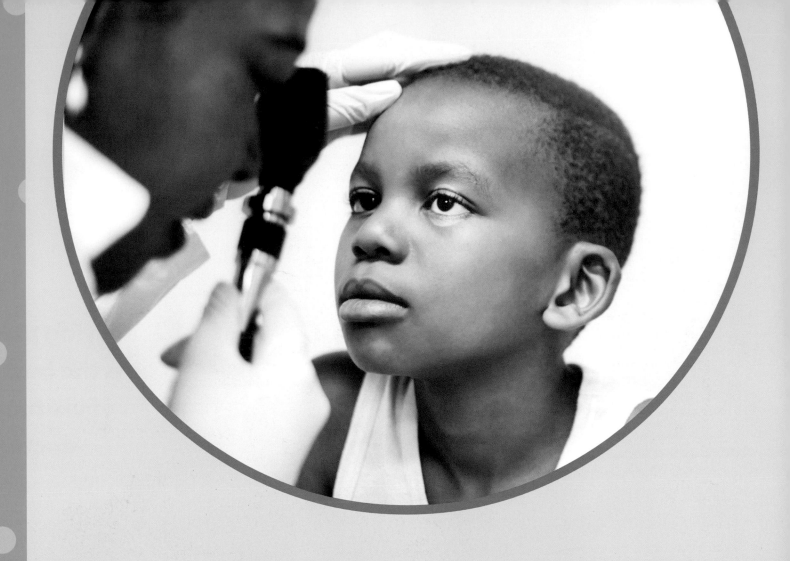

Doctors use a small light to look in your eyes.

They check your muscles and bones.

I, Super Grover, have strong muscles.

Sometimes doctors give you medicines. Some medicines make sick people better.

I'm brave when it's time for a shot. It only pinches for a minute.

Some medicines stop people from getting sick.

Doctors listen when patients ask questions.
Doctors help us learn how to stay healthy.

25

Doctors need to work as a team.

They work hard to help their patients.

Thank You, Doctors!

Now's it's your turn. Write a thank-you letter to your doctor.

Dear Doctor,

Thank you for keeping everyone in my community healthy. I am glad you know how to make me feel better.

Your friend,

Big Bird

Picture Glossary

checkup: a doctor visit to find out if the patient is healthy

community: a place where people live and work

healthy: not sick or injured

medicines: things taken to make people feel better or to keep them from getting sick

Read More

Driscoll, Laura. *I Want to Be a Doctor.* New York: Harper, 2018.

Heos, Bridget. *Doctors in My Community.* Minneapolis: Lerner Publications, 2019.

Waxman, Laura Hamilton. *Doctor Tools.* Minneapolis: Lerner Publications, 2020.

Index

Photo Acknowledgments

Additional image credits: ER Productions Limited/Getty Images, p. 5; andresr/Getty Images, pp. 6, 30; Morsa Images/Getty Images, p. 7; FatCamera/Getty Images, pp. 8, 25; Weekend Images Inc./Getty Images, p. 9; Maskot/Getty Images, p. 10; SDI Productions/Getty Images, pp. 11, 30; Steve Hix/Fuse/Getty Images, p. 12; Hero Images/Getty Images, pp. 13, 16–17, 26; monkeybusinessimages/Getty Images, p. 14; ADAM GAULT/SPL/Getty Images, p. 15; Hybrid Images/Getty Images, p. 18; Terry Vine/Getty Images, p. 19; mapodile/Getty Images, p. 20; KidStock/Getty Images, p. 21; Sam Edwards/Getty Images, pp. 22, 30; fstop123/Getty Images, p. 23; Jose Luis Pelaez Inc/Getty Images, pp. 24, 30; LightFieldStudios/Getty Images, p. 27; NanoStockk/Getty Images, p. 29.

Cover: Tetra Images/Getty Images.

Lerner Publications Company
An imprint of Lerner Publishing Group, Inc.
241 First Avenue North
Minneapolis, MN 55401 USA

For reading levels and more information, look up this title at www.lernerbooks.com.

Main body text set in Mikado Medium.
Typeface provided by HVD Fonts.

Editor: Allison Juda **Designer:** Emily Harris **Photo Editor:** Rebecca Higgins
Lerner team: Martha Kranes, Katy Prozinski

Library of Congress Cataloging-in-Publication Data

Names: Boothroyd, Jennifer, 1972- author.
Title: All about doctors / Jennifer Boothroyd.
Description: Minneapolis : Lerner Publications, [2021] | Series: Sesame Street loves community helpers | Includes bibliographical references and index. | Audience: Ages 4–8 | Audience: Grades K–1 | Summary: "Big Bird knows doctors keep him healthy and strong. Join Big Bird and the rest of the Sesame Street cast as they celebrate these important community helpers!"– Provided by publisher.
Identifiers: LCCN 2019037081 (print) | LCCN 2019037082 (ebook) | ISBN 9781541589964 (library binding) | ISBN 9781728400921 (ebook)
Subjects: LCSH: Physicians—Vocational guidance—Juvenile literature.
Classification: LCC R690 .B644 2021 (print) | LCC R690 (ebook) | DDC 610.69/5–dc23

LC record available at https://lccn.loc.gov/2019037081
LC ebook record available at https://lccn.loc.gov/2019037082

Manufactured in the United States of America
1-47506-48050-11/20/2019